Petite Rouge

A Cajun Twist to An Old Tale

Sheila Hébert Collins
11-8-94

Blue Heron Press

Story: Sheila Hébert Collins
Illustrations: Chris Diket

Blue Heron Press
P.O. Box 550
Thibodaux, LA 70302
(504) 446-8201

Printed in the United States of America

ISBN 1-884725-02-3

ISBN 1-884725-02-3
51495>
9 781884 725029

Petite Rouge

A Cajun Twist to An Old Tale

By Sheila Hébert Collins

Illustrated by Chris Diket

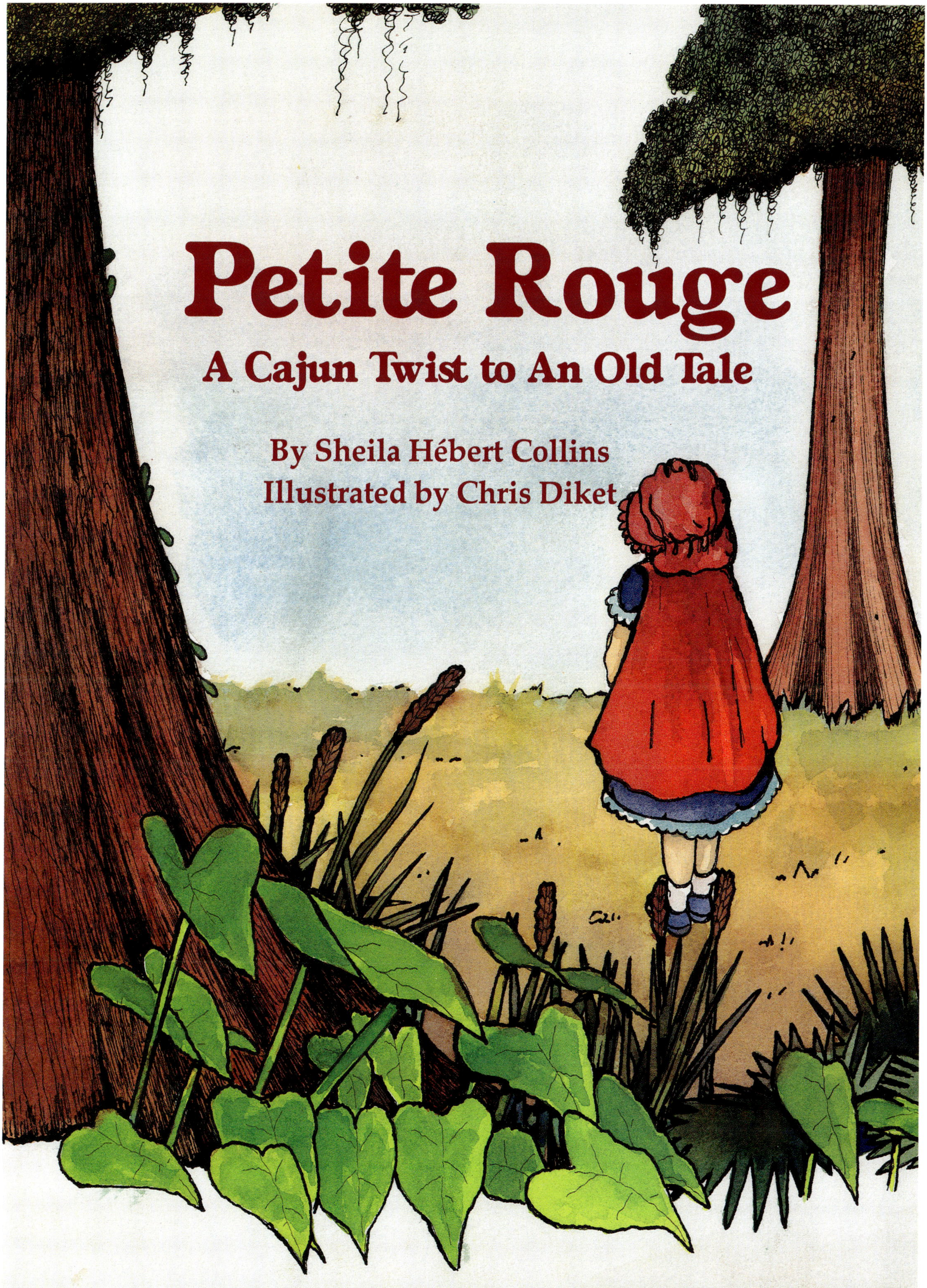

A Note to the Storyteller

To assist you in correctly pronouncing
the Cajun French words in this story book,
the following pronounciation guide is provided.

ã	face
ah	hot
ee	teeth
air	bear
oo	toot
õ	boat
u	up
o	log
oñ	"o" nasal
eñ	"i" nasal
e	let
a	at
ç	c sound as in pass
ü	uh (aspirated)
ä	a sound as in pear
j	g sound as in germ

Dedication

This book is dedicated to

Lillian Mouton Hébert

- mother of Cordell, Reid,
Byron, Joey and Sheila;

grandmother of thirteen and
great-grandmother of four
- at this time.

She leads her "sheep" with
love, patience, and compassion.
She is loved and appreciated
by her entire "flock."

Once upon a time there was a family named Mouton. They lived on Bayou Tigre near the town of Delcambre in South Louisiana.

Mouton (moo-toñ) - A Cajun family name meaning sheep

Bayou Tigre (by-yoo teeg) - A small stream near Delcambre

Delcambre (del-come) - A small, shrimping and fishing community in south Louisiana

Clotilde was the only daughter of Clodis and Odelia. Papa Clodis was a shrimp-*trawler* who worked hard in the bayous near Delcambre, while Mama Odelia stayed home mending trawls, cooking, and sewing.

Clotilde (Clo teel) - A good Cajun name for a girl

trawler (troller) - A person who uses a trawl(net) for shrimping

Clodis (Clö dees) - A good Cajun name for a man

Odelia (Oh deel yah) - A good Cajun name for a woman

Having only one daughter, Odelia enjoyed making her petite Clotilde pretty clothes. Clotilde's favorite outfit was one Mother had made for the big *fais do do* the night before *Mardi Gras*. It had a beautiful red cloak with a matching *garde-soleil*. She wore it so often that she became known up and down the bayou as *Petite Rouge*. (Some *Américains* called her Little Red Riding Hood.)

---

fais do do (fay doe doe) - A street or barn dance lasting late into the night.

Mardi Gras (mar-dee grah) - "Fat Tuesday," a day of celebration before the first day of Lent, Ash Wednesday.

garde-soleil (guard so-lay) - sunbonnet • Petite Rouge (p'teet rooj) - "Little Red"

Amèricains (ah-mair-ee-kahn) - Cajuns once referred to anyone who spoke English as Américains.

One fall evening, Clotilde's mother made a shrimp *etouffée* for *Grandmère* Mouton. *Grandmère* lived across the bayou about a mile away. Mother called out, "Clotilde, *vien ici!* Take dis *etouffée* to *Grandmère* Mouton. She took sick yesterday, *pauve bête.*"

---

etouffée (a-too-fay) - a rich stew

Grandmère (groñ-mare) - grandmother

vien ici (vee-yehn ee-see) - come here

pauvre bête (pawv bet) - poor thing

"Put on your *garde-soleil* and cape so you don't take a chill from dat fog. And be careful, yeah! Watch for dat big gator *taille-taille!*"

---

garde-soleil (gard so-lay) - sunbonnet

taille - taille (tie - tie) - a monster, a huge alligator

Petite Rouge crossed the bayou in her *pirogue* and began the long walk through the dark swamp.

---

pirogue (pee-rogue) - a small boat made of cypress.

Not very far from the bayou, Clotilde met a big gator. She looked very closely at the gator. Could this be the big gator *taille-taille* Mother had warned her about? *Mais non!* He looked too friendly!

---

taille-taille (tie-tie) - a monster, a huge alligator

mais non (mä noñ) - but, no

Ah bien, pauvre Petite Rouge.
She didn't know that gator would have gobbled her up
right then and there except he heard the shrimpboats coming in,
so he didn't dare.

---

ah bien (ah be-ehn) - oh, well

pauvre (pa-vre) - poor

That smart gator knew this was the time of day when many trawlers would be cleaning and hanging their trawls. And *chere pitié!* what a feast he would make if those trawlers caught him!

chère pitie' (sha pee-tay) - dear pity

"*Bonsoir, petite fille,*" said that gator in a smoothe, friendly voice.
"And where would you be going on dis foggy evenin'?"
he asked ever so nicely.

---

bonsoir (boñ-swah) - good evening

petite fille (p'teet fee) - little girl

"I'm going to my *Grandmère's* 'cross de swamp," Petite Rouge answered sweetly, still not suspecting this was the gator *taille-taille* her mother had warned her about.

•

She went on talking.
"*Grandmère* lives in de first house pas' de Delcambre bridge. She's not feeling very well, so my Mother made her this good shrimp *etoufée*."

---

etoufée (a-too-fay) - a rich stew

"Mais, *ça c'est tris!* I'll go *veillee,* too!" said that *gros menteur.* "You take dat way, I'll take dis way and we'll see who gets dere first. *Dépêche-toi!*"

---

mais ça c'est tris (may, sah say tree) - now that's a shame

veillee (vä yä) - to stay and visit in the evening

gros menteur (grow men-tour) - horrible monster

dépêche-toi (day pesh twâh) - hurry up

Of course, that gator knew his way around that swamp better than Petite Rouge so he found *Grandmère's* house *tout de suite.* He knocked on the door.

tout de suite (toot sweet) - quickly, right away

"Who's dere?" *Grandmère* called out weakly.

"It's your Petite Rouge, Clotilde," said that gator *taille-taille,* making his voice sound almost like Clotilde's. He was a real *flatteur,* him!

flatteur (flâ-ter) - a flatterer

Grandmère, who couldn't hear too well and couldn't get out of bed anyway, called out:
"Pull de string, cher, and de latch will come open."
Well, the gator pulled the string, the door flew open, and before you could say "hot *boudoin*" he gobbled her up!
Then he put on *Grandmère's tignon* and *camisole*

---

hot boudoin (boo dehñ) - A Cajun sausage made with rice and meat.

tignon (tee yon) - kerchief

camisole (cam ee sol) - a lady's nightgown

...got in that bed ...and waited for Petite Rouge.

Soon there came a-tapping at the door. "Who's dere?" called the gator, trying to sound as much like *Grandmère* as he could.

Petite Rouge was frightened by the hoarse voice,
but then she thought,
"It must by the *mal de gourge* that makes her sound so bad."
"Quoi ça dis?" asked Clotilde.

"Who's dere at my door?" repeated the gator,
this time sounding even more like *Grandmère*.

"It's your own Petite Rouge, *Grandmère*.
I brought you some good shrimp *etouffée*," answered Clotilde.

"Pull de string, cher, and de latch will come loose," said the gator.

Petite Rouge pulled the string, the door opened, and in she went.

That gator *taille-taille* slid further under the covers and said,
"Put de *etouffée* on de stove, *cher*, and *vien ici*."

Petite Rouge put down the *etouffée*, walked over to the bed and sat on the edge. She was so surprised to see how strange *Grandmère* looked.

"Pooh-yi!" she thought, "What a *grimace*!
Grandmère really must be sick!"

Petite Rouge looked more closely at *Grandmère*.

---

mal de gourge (mah der gorj) - sore throat

Quoi ça dis (quaw sah dee) - What did you say?

vien ici (vee-yehn ee-see) - come here

pooh yi (poo-yee) - A Cajun expression meaning "Oh, my!"

grimace (gree-mahs) - an ugly face

"Grandmère!" she said, "What big arms you got!"
"De better to hug you wit, *mon cheri,*" the gator replied.

---

mon cheri (moñ sherrie) - my pretty

"*Grandmère!*" exclaimed Petite Rouge,
"What big eyes you got!"
"De better to see my Petite Rouge," said the gator in a nervous voice.
"But *Grandmère!*" screamed Petite Rouge, "What great teet you got!"
"De better to eat you wit, *mon ami!*" growled that gator *taille-taille!*

With that, the big gator jumped out of bed and
gobbled up Petite Rouge!

•

That's the way some say the story ends,
but people up and down Bayou Tigre swear the shrimpers heard Petite Rouge screaming and came running to help her.

---

mon ami (moñ ah me) - my friend

Once they got to *Grandmère's* house they found that big gator *taille-taille,* cut open his bulging belly and out stepped *Grandmère* and Petite Rouge — whole and fine!

The shrimpers then cooked up that gator *taille-taille* and made the best alligator *sauce piquante* you ever could eat!

sauce piquant (sauce pee kahnt) - spicey, red gravy

When they finished supper, they all went to a big *fais do do* and passed a good time!
C'est toute!!

c'est toute (say too) - that's all

ALLIGATOR SAUCE PIQUANTE

Ingredients:

2 lbs of pre-cooked gator meat
(cubed chicken or fish,any meat or fish will do)
(season with salt and cayenne before cooking)
1 finely chopped bellpepper
1 finely chopped large onion
1 finely chopped garlic clove
2 finely chopped stalks of celery
8 oz. fresh mushrooms (chopped)
1/2 cup of vegetable oil
1 can rotel tomatoes (diced)
2 - 4oz cans of tomato sauce
1 can of tomato paste + 1 can of water
1 tablespoon of worschestire sauce
1 bay leaf
1/4 cup onion tops and parsley
1 teaspoon Tabasco Sauce (optional)

Directions:

Saute vegetables in oil.
Add rotel tomatoes and 1 can of tomato paste to one can of water
Add two cans of tomato sauce
Add bay leaf and worschestire sauce
Simmer 45 minutes.
Add precooked meat and simmer an additional 20 minutes.
(Pre-cook meat by frying in small amount of oil and drain)
Add 1/4 cup of onion tops and parsley before serving.
Serve over steamed rice.
Bon Appetite!

Bon Appetite (boñ ah-p'teet) - Eat well, enjoy your food